Random Adventures

Also by Martin Christmas and published by Ginninderra Press
Immediate Reflections (Picaro Poets)
The Deeper Inner (Pocket Poets)
D&M Between 2 Men (with Andrew Drake)

Martin Christmas
Random Adventures

Thanks

To the high school teacher who said I was thick; would never need English; and shoved me into bookkeeping! He lit a fire within. The same year, the high school magazine printed the first poem I ever wrote.

To Friendly Street Poets, who published a four-line poem in their *Reader 36* back in 2012.

To Jules Leigh Koch, who was my Friendly Street Poets mentor and encouraged me to develop strong poetic imagery.

To Rob Walker and his *Persist!* mantra that has driven me since 2015.

To Michelle Hartman, former editor of *Red River Review*, Texas, USA, who had enough faith in my work to name me Featured Poet for Autumn 2018.

To Stephen and Brenda Matthews at Ginninderra Press. Their encouragement of local poets is legendary.

And to you, the readers of poetry, who are willing to go on random adventures from page to page to…

Random Adventures
ISBN 978 1 76041 816 8
Copyright © text Martin Christmas 2019
Copyright © cover photo and internal photos Martin Christmas 2019

First published 2019 by
GINNINDERRA PRESS
PO Box 3461 Port Adelaide 5015
www.ginninderrapress.com.au

Contents

Random Adventures	9
Outback ruin	10
Chatting with Fellini	12
Alfresco dining	14
Bins	16
Intimate Theatre	18
Marduk & Mark	19
Evicted Splendour	20
So too with friendship	21
Killer Assault Course	23
Not quite Villers-Bretonneux	25
Close Encounter	28
CBD Reality	31
No Through Road	33
How does the saying go?	34
Fifteen Pelicans	37
Wet Present	39
Straw hat upwardly mobile	41
Ya, ya, ya	43
254 to Dreamtime	46
Blue to Brown	48
Western Suburb Heaven	49
Sexy Brick Wall	52
By the light, but not the silvery moon	54
Chainsaw Massacre	56
Angel Face	59
Cruising Industrial Fortresses	62
Sunset Industries	63
I'm sorry, sir, I'm a bit slow	65
Old woman, blue coat	66

They should shoot people like me	68
Diamonds not forever	71
Ad Victor Spolia	72
First splashes	74
Unnatural Assignation	76
Dunny Snake	80
Sheep Eyes	82
Seven thousand tigers	84
Standing in the pit	86
The Spanning Years	88
Father and Son	90
And burnt to death	93
At times like this	95
Unending Sadness	97
In Australia, my voice identifies me	99
Natural Selection	102
Loo break with Aunty ABC	103
Vale ladder	105
Small Egos Travelling	107
Small Life Force Voyager	108
Acknowledgements	109
About the Author	110

Random Adventures

Neither here not there
but anywhere
and in between.

Outback ruin,
CBD reality.
Wet present
and 254 to dreamtime.
Western suburb heaven.

A sexy brick wall,
chainsaw massacre,
sheep eyes and tigers.
Unending sadness.
A loo break with Aunty ABC
and much more.

We are all small life force
voyagers.
Everyday. Every way.

Random adventures
are all around us.

Outback ruin

Hot sun, cloudless sky.
As far the eye sees, flat empty plain.
The track threads its lonely way to
the shimmering horizon.

The merciless sun drums the mulga bush.
On one side of the endless track,
a homestead
slowly crumbling into dust.

Roof long since caved in,
snapped and rotten timbers
for an occasional magpie
or galah to nest in.

Empty window frame socket rattles.
Small ripple wind, harp sings
and courts the old almond tree
beside the window frame.

This tuneful little wind turns,
seeking a way out of the maze
of rubbled sandstone,
finds a small hole in the one complete wall,
squeezes through,
tumbles down the path.

Out through the wicker gate it goes.
The wind is free, and whisks off
across the purple plain
as the crumbling ruin
returns to silent peace,
again.

Chatting with Fellini

Rocked up early for a meeting with a friend
at a wood oven pizza place, warm in
winter, on the road to Adelaide.

This little man with over his collar grey hair,
sits in a corner, by a flashy gilded mirror,
wearing a fedora hat and black-rimmed glasses.

There's Marilyn and Elvis and Charlie. Audrey
and Harrison and Clark and Vivian (Leigh).
Tomorrow is another day, 8½ weeks from spring.

The place near empty. Well used tables, chairs.
Wooden. If they could speak, what stories tell,
but for another time, or maybe after midnight.

He flashes a serious smile. We talk.
Italian. I once emailed to Barcelona University
in Google Spanish, re-translated, it was crap,

so keep my side to '*si*' and '*si*' as he emotes.
His name is Federico, seems he'd
made a film or four. He knew his stuff.

Those earlier spoken of certainly knew of him,
though I doubt they'd ever found their marks
on his film sets, and certainly not Elvis.

The King and Marilyn were busy anyway, as
they flirted near my table. Harrison the voyeur
had his whip out, and was raiding a lost ark.

My friend arrived. M, E, C, A, H, C (Gable) and V,
stepped back onto the walls. Gone with the wind.
I turned to Federico, but only an empty chair.

He'd left the room before I could convey how
I had enjoyed his films *Satyricon* and *8½*
all those years ago, when life was simpler.

Fellini's. Great cappuccinos, pizzas.

Alfresco dining

The ad read,
'Outside ambience.
Hindmarsh Square.
Handy parking.
Formal table settings.
Grate surroundings.'

The whole team turned up.
What a spread.
Amazing pizza.
Ample serves
for all of us.

The long silver thingy
was unnecessary.
When in Rome
eat pizza with your fingers,
whatever.
The match was handy
to scale the box.
Ant-hony and his crew
replaced it by the thingy,
as you would.

But grate meal.
No waiters hassled us
to finish or move on.
Grate food. Grate service,
all 200 of us agreed.

Star rating: 4.
We'll certainly come again.
Ant-icipate many more
when the message gets around,
'Alfresco dining in the Square,
the way to go.'

Grate!

Bins

All week
they engorge themselves
regardless
of their waistlines,
blood vessels.

Some demure,
others gaudy.
Broken, grubby,
weathered, scarred,
spiderwebbed.

Deadly aroma
takes the breath
away. Sitting slyly
side by side
by house side.

Then rushed
to kerbside, suddenly.
They wait, they wait,
till, across the suburbs,
they vomit, anorexic like.

All done
until next week's Solo
truck arrives.

Intimate Theatre

A tall muscular man
with vibrant silky hair
sits in the stalls nearby.
His partner, much slighter,
and with glasses.

He puts his hand on
his partner's thigh,
who covers it with his
jumper.
Thus they enjoyed the show
as one,
and afterwards,
leave
quickly.

Marduk & Mark

Reading *The Babylon Creation*
circa 12th century BC,
in awe, I hesitate.

Marduk & his battle with
the evil she god Tiamut,
all blood & guts & death.

Spielberg would have done it proud.
A long gone past informs us yet,
as old as humankind, is love, is hate.

Today, across the road,
my 10 years neighbour, Mark,
packed his ute & trailer & left (with dog).
Quick final handshake,
'The differences have widened.'
A wife & grown kids left behind.

Mark is no god Marduk,
just an ordinary man.

Hate. Debate. Hesitate. Exasperate.

Terminate.

Evicted Splendour

(as Lord Byron might have writ, or maybe not)

Beneath the yellow plastic tape,
I languish silent here.
Once, so enjoyed, but now
a tawdry cold crime scene,
and not IKEA.

My faded silken splendour,
if I could shed a tear,
cold, depleted, naked,
abandoned, but still dear.

A seat of joy, of love,
no memories to perturb.
Now all alone, alone
entrapped, on this isolated kerbside.

All of us were great once,
our end is never clear.
Centre of the lounge room
one week, now the tip,
I fear.

So too with friendship

All seems tight when setting out.

Sometimes along the way, though,
members of the expedition
veer off
in new directions.

If one calls, 'Keep together',
it all seems false
and aims and energies
are lost in careless conflict.

So too with friendship.

We sense a separation of the ways.
To bind together
makes the wounded animal see red.
Better to say, 'Goodbye'
on a firm handshake.

So too with friendship.

The reaching of a summit,
old flags flown.
Eyes strain forward
barely seeing
distant peaks
beyond.

New flags.
New peaks.
The expedition counts its losses,
and moves on.

Killer Assault Course

is ready for its first
commandos to be toughened
up. There will be
broken bones for sure.

The shiny blue ejector ring sits
over red cement so that
you won't see the blood
oozing from your leg.

The cute bouncy horse
will throw you forward
or squeeze your toes inside
its awesome spring.

Boulders cunningly placed
and siren calling,
'Land on us,
we'll rip your skin.
Only a matter of time before
we rock you   literally.'

Lastly, the assault tower
fingering the sky,
urging you upwards
spiderweb like,
higher, higher, 'Look at me,
look at me   ahhhh,'   as you
fall to the ground and crack
your spine.

A high-vis worker does a crash dummy run
with a real young kid on the shiny blue
ejector ring. The kid is screaming.
His white balloon just broke.

The course is ready for commandos.

Only a matter of time before a mum
calls triple zero, 'Please come.
Billy's not breathing, maybe dead.
He's my eight-year-old son.
He landed on his head.'

Not quite Villers-Bretonneux

Heavy fighting on the front.
Containment at least
till reinforcements
come.

Wave after wave of
enemy troops
pour from
their trenches.

You have to admire
their tenacity.
No, damn it!
They are the enemy
and everyone
of them must be
stopped at all costs.
Hold on! Hold on!
Reinforcements
will come, what hope?
The day is lost.

Small victories.
A lull.
Then they pour out
of their trenches
once again,
determined to scale the
heights.

Hundreds die and yet
still come.
Tenacious buggers.
Damn them!

They are swept away
and still they come.
Call in the Big Gun.
Mineral Turps.
Success for a
few minutes.
Stillness.

Silence

The dying in the trenches.
The end, or so it seems.

But one more time
again they build their
numbers, start to scale
the heights. Swept away,
only to return.

There will not be another day!

Off to Bunnings
for some
ant rid powder.

Damn their
tenacity!

I will not be
defeated
by these ants
swarming up
the back wall of
the house!

Total ant-ihilation
begins
when I return!

Close Encounter

Utter carnage.
The footbridge
felled by heavy machinery.

Twisted light poles
melted by death rays
across the Torrens.

Montefiore Drive strewn with
burnt out car shells.
Dying men, women, children.
Oh the humanity!
No *Hindenburg* airship mishap
but bloody calculated
all out destruction.

The Festival Centre destroyed.
One chilling blast.
The Casino not far behind.
Exploding North Terrace towers.
Even Holy Trinity Church
not protected by God's intervention.

Double take.
Full moon.
No *War of the Worlds*
mind game aberration,
or was it?

All quiet
on the parklands front.
Serene. Clear.
Starry starry night.

Just the Adelaide Oval stadium
doing its nightly light show.
Nothing to call home about.

CBD Reality

A constant two-way
flow of people.
Where are they going?
Where have they been?
Street people
moving somewhere
through the CBD
reality frame.

The old musician
strums his guitar,
amplified softly, battling
against the Subway music
box, and news that the
big game at the stadium begins
in 30 minutes!

Still they come with that pace
that determines they are not beach
walkers drifting, but committed
pram pushers, bag carriers.
Commuters on the
treadmill of CBD travellers
between nowhere and a
somewhere
known only to them.

A classic orange Ford
Mustang screams towards
the traffic lights.

Vroom! Vroom!

'The Sound of Silence'
via Disturbed, echoes
from the Subway music box.

Nothing
stops the reality of the endless flow.

No Through Road

The stench of diesel fuel
assails the nostrils.
Bus after bus idles,
picking up
the standing trade.

CBD Adelaide.

T-shirt scribbles
by the score.
Go Round – wobbly breasts.
Oakley – tall and skinny guy.
88 – schoolboy in casuals.

Stilettos, sandals,
thongs, joggers,
formal blacks and sockless.
Suits and suits
and frocks and frocks.

Phones, earplugs.
Fixed stares everywhere.
Crunch of brakes.
Tough, focused, heading
somewhere.
Not a no through road,
but home.

A homeless man
lying on a bench
in Gilbert Place.
No home to go to,
just a No Through Road.

How does the saying go?

'Walk a mile in another man's shoes.'

Hard to do if the other man staring at you
is standing under a pub awning
sheltering from the rain
as you turn his corner
in your burgundy Toyota Lexcen.
He has no shoes.

Bare toes curling the wet cement.
He stares at you through
his blond matted hair
as he shelters in thin clothes
as you in your burgundy Toyota Lexcen
listen to a live concert on ABC Classic FM
(I think it was Beethoven's Symphony Number 3
in E Flat.
Eroica, the 2nd movement).

10.15 p.m.
Cold. Drizzling rain.
You drive to your safe house,
a warm bed, and he,
cold cement
        curled up.

Turn the electric blanket on, and he,
and you, and he.

Hard to swap footwear
when the man in the headlights
stares at you as you turn
his corner
>> his space
>> >> his world.

He has no shoes,
his eyes already dead.

Fifteen Pelicans

Unspectacular distant specks
heading for Outer Harbor,
and sailors home from a race,
caressing their crafts onto trailers.

The dying end of spring.

The specks in the sky expand,
not seagulls heading home,
but pelicans.

Fifteen pelicans.

Coming for a long hot summer.
Tourists gliding in
from somewhere else.

The sailors busy their fingers,
busy their minds.

The pelicans glide closer,
their graceful manoeuvres
appealing as any corps de ballet.

The sailors continue to push;
shoving their groaning
charges shorewards.

Pelicans.

Gliding overhead now,
their bodies etched
individually, and yet;
part of a living breathing being.
Pink, white, grey,
flapping in rhythmic sync
ripple formation.
A sensitive piece of aerial
gymnastics.

Sailors' hands are stilled.
Humans and birds bonding
for a few precious moments.

Sympatico.

The pelicans flap, wheel,
making their way along the coast.
Programmed. Silent passage.
Timeless presence.

No flock of Qantas 787s comes near
the grace of these fifteen pelicans.

A wave breaks across the shore.
The sailors return to their labours.

Fifteen pelicans have arrived.
Summer is here.
The pelicans have packed
their sunsuits.

Wet Present

'Here's ya jacket, mate. Get into it.'

I stumble forward
looking at the cruel sea,
wincing but determined
to go the full distance.

'If I misjudge the waves out,
don't get caught as she tips.'

Profoundly I think of insurance,
a broken leg maybe.
I'd only come down
for a bit of a chat.

'Let's go, get on NOW,
and keep well back. Who knows?'

The Cat shoots through the surf
straight from Hell's vortex.
Every wave across the bow
drenching us to the bone.

'If she goes over, slide off,
and don't get caught up if ya can help it.'

At the eight-minute mark
we are tacking about,
moving fast, barrelling,
vaulting, gathering speed.

'Bloody hell!' my constant
comment most of the trip back.

At the fifteen-minute mark
we sweep fast onto
surf sodden sand

'Happy birthday, mate.'

Best bloody present for years,
what a way to 'break a leg'.

Straw hat upwardly mobile

Sultry waves crash on the exhausted beach.
Seagulls chant their eerie cry.
Gusts of wind push on my face.

Damn! My favourite straw hat
upwardly mobile and scudding towards
a watery death, leapfrogging the sand.

I follow like a late tourist,
feet scrunching the hot grains,
vain effort to stop the inevitable.

Thongs, sun cream, glasses, towel, keys.
All of us in hot pursuit,
following the jewel in the crown.

My favourite straw hat. Hero.
Sun service in the heat of the Riverland,
the brown dust of the Mallee.
Many a coach journey scrunched up
ready at a moments notice to
fight the murderous UVRs.

To end its glorious service in the Outlet,
skimming along, now out of sight.

Running feet in pursuit,
over the rise, I see it floating,
Titanic-like, majestic still,
halfway across the murky channel.
Abandon ship!

Cursing the hot wind, I run faster,
watching this beloved macho symbol
going down at the head band.

No music sounds a last farewell,
no lifeboats lowered,
and by the time a rescue is at hand,
sunk, with all straws.

Thrusting my way through the scum,
risking needles and condoms,
arriving at the water's edge,
searching for the corpse
to pay my last respects.
Found it!

Submerged, silent, silenced.
Soggy, it lifts in my fingers
dripping weeds, but intact, safe,
just a leeetle bit damp.
I gather it up like a diamond found,
and push home to a reviving tap.

All rinsed out and sitting cocky
on the room divide. The miracle.
Dried off, it's ready to head out again.

Upwardly mobile, jaunty.
There's a hundred outings yet
in that old straw hat.

You can't keep a good hat down!

Ya, ya, ya

Lady, early 80s, white hair, crinkly face, lipstick.
I imagine her, early 20s, Eastern European
dazzler back in the early 50s.
She clutches a blue shopping bag
waiting for the 10.05 a.m. bus.
A good morning to shop.

Ilka, well that's the name I imagine her
being, stands, shields her eyes,
looks up the road, 'Vil it evar come?'
Maybe Ilka was a tennis player in Budapest.
No bus comes. 'Been waiting long?'
Ilka, '*Ya, ya, ya.*'

'Sit,' I say. 'The bus will come eventually.'
She, 'I don't vant to sit!' and questions
the wisdom of living by a main road.
I reply, '*Ya, ya, ya.*'

She sits. We wait. She stands.
She looks for 'our bus'. Good eyesight,
sporty shades atop her crinkly white hair.
I see the 20s-something Budapest tennis player.
Stunning. Greta Garbo couldn't
have done it better. I nearly say,
'You vont to be alone?' but miss the moment.
Maybe Ilka is Swedish.

She sees our bus a few stops away.
'Vil it stop for us?' I say, 'If not,
I will leap into the road and hijack it.'
'*Ya, ya, ya* cheeky man. I will punch your body!'
I say, '*Ya, ya, ya.*'
We laugh simultaneously.
She gets on. I get on.

'You would have been great to make love to
back in 1953 at the Café Ruszwurm in Budapest.'
'*Ya, ya, ya*, in ya dreams, buster!'

In my imagination, Ilka.

254 to Dreamtime

9.15 p.m. Adelaide Festival Centre.
254 to Port Adelaide.

Plump Aboriginal woman sits quietly
on cement slab beside the bus stop.

Bus arrives. The woman boards, sits next
to a young Australian, could be Greek.

Loud group of Africans jump on board.
One steps on her naked foot.
She makes no sound.

Suddenly, the Africans exit,
'Wrong bloody bus!' The woman sits quietly.

She wears a Rainbow Serpent dress.
Her brown feet strangely out of place,
foreign, even.

Later.

Her head rests on the young man's shoulder.
He ignores it, looks out the window.

Gently she sinks further into his body.
His look of horror speaks loudly.
Her head now cemented to his side. Dreamtime.

Later.

Halfway to Port Adelaide, he nudges her awake,
squeezes past, exits by the middle door.
She struggles to her feet, exits by the driver's door.

Both into the darkness.
Two strangers united by a bus ride.
Moment of cultural connection

lost.

Blue to Brown

Turn the corner,
nearly home.

Cement shade sitting,
Aboriginal elder, gum tree gazing.

'Spare two dollar?'

'Nothing on me. Sorry.'
He eats chips from a plastic bowl.

Later, I return. He still sits stoically.
'Ten dollars be OK?'

He nods a yes.
Eyes connect. Blue to brown.

I shake his hand.
'Your country first.'

Western Suburb Heaven

Magpie on oval
eyeing seagull sentinels
standing silent
as council mower
drones on
cuttingly.

Yellow-vested
workmen replace
roofing on
community hall.
Go the Hawks!

Four light posts
stand tall.
Soccer. Footy.
Night-time sports.

Steady traffic hum
on Hanson Road.
Trucks, cars, buses.

Heartbeat thumps.
Someone plays
African music.
Local pro solicits sex
in broad daylight.

Melaleucas,
bottlebrushes, gums,
offer their shade.
Incessant rasp of
myna birds.
Above all, wispy
clouds drift through
a pale blue sky.

Western suburb heaven?

Breath of God ruffles the hair
on the back of my neck.

Sexy Brick Wall

5 months ago,
down came 7 metres
of early 60s rusted corrugated iron
fencing much to my disgust.
Fence rape by the owner of
the property next door.
A new garage for the new units
was his excuse.

The 7-metre gap
remained temporary
fencing.

November	no garage wall.
December	likewise.
January	the same.
February	a garage frame goes up.

Last week,
7 a.m., a cool morning,
4 Italian workmen arrived to
build The Wall.

Within 3 days
the garage wall was up.
7 metres of neat brick wall. More than neat.
Sexy. Why?

Handcrafted, brick by brick,
mortar layer by mortar layer,
33 bricks long by 30 bricks high.
Do the maths. Each placed with
precise craftsmanship,
washed down lovingly at the end
of each day's work,
Monday to Wednesday.

4 guys, craftsmen every one.
A sexy garage wall, 990 bricks
in all, and matching the older
existing house. Suddenly,
total privacy. What's more,
a noise buffer from the dull thud
of the Hanson Road traffic
day and night. Sexy, very.

How damn sexy must it have been
to watch the building of the Great
Wall of China or the Pyramids of Giza?

By the light, but not the silvery moon

Blackout. Almost evening.
Sirens sound on Hanson Road.
Rush of wind through trees.
Thunder rolls. Light rain
on the front slate path.

I write this poem by
the light of the trusty
Luminator lantern
bought some years ago
and used so many times
since then. A dear friend.

Sound of silence, or more
the hum of traffic.
Low bird calls.
Windows rattling lightly
in the wind. Storm passing.

Funny moment for a blackout.
Preparing some new poems
for a poetry read
at an open mic poetry event.

By the steady glow, not gas
nor candle even,
I could be Victor Hugo,
but don't speak French,
or Adrianus writing *Alexandriad*
(if I wrote Greek).
So in the Athens of the South,
a quick poem in the gloom.

Things could be worse. Like
Goya's soldier on the stump
ramrodded up the bum.

Time for tea and start
a magic journey to the past,
but not to be.
Sixty minutes later,
everything lights up.
Romantic journey thuds
to a resounding halt.
Normality returns.
This chance for
Paradise
is lost.

Chainsaw Massacre

The instrument of Death is spied,
then bought, and loaded
in the boot. No strip search,
police car siren, ASIO report,
just loaded in the boot,
with anticipation of what murder
lay ahead.

'Read the instructions carefully,'
the manual said. I did, I did, I did
again, until in fear,
I set aside my task, my deadly task,
and father confessed to Facebook
friends who warned me of
electrocution, decapitation,
kickback, not the political kind,
but chainsaw hitting obstacle, and going
for the jugular, not wood, my head.
An avalanche of fears released.

Step one was done, and then step two,
involving putting on the chain.
Almost sweated blood to make the
job as good as poss, so that
injury or death (mine),
didn't happen on my watch.

Then an inner voice yelled,
'Do it now!
Don't put it off till after lunch.'
And donning goggles, ear protectors, work gloves,
gumboots, and looking like an
astronaut or some weird ghoul,
I began the task, the bloody task itself.

Set the instrument of Death in place;
filled the oil sump; connected cable
from the house; hooked in the extension cord;
took a safe position on flat ground.

Prepare to meet thy doom!

The innocent tree stump
lay silent just ahead and unaware it's
cutting fate. The old hand saw
bemoaned its loss of kingship in the shed.

One final check of printed words;
turned on the power; three deep breaths;
pressed the red button.
The instrument of Death alive,
fast rips into the screaming wood.
The chainsaw massacre commenced.

Fifteen minutes of total fearful focus,
concentration, following instruction
imprinted in my head,
cutting with abandon, cactus wood,
whatever came my way.

Chainsaw virginity is lost.
Orgasmic pleasure moment,
dripping sweat,
such macho primitive release.

An end for now. Enough.
Lunchtime, but thinking,
'If I were more unhinged,
I might search out more deadly
cut and thrust.'

This chainsaw massacre stuff
is fun.

I only lost
three fingers

     and a thumb!

Angel Face

Buying apples, local green grocers.
Battle protagonists: Filipino assistant and
angel-faced blond Aussie, fifteen years or so.

'I'm taking these,'
clutching the goods tight to his young chest,
marching to the
checkout counter barrier.

My heart goes out.
Young and broke, maybe an offer to pay?
Pull back, listen longer
as the Filipino guy calls the police.

'I'm taking these!' Louder,
but a bargain struck.
'I won't be back!'
Defiant harassment aimed.
Picked up, diplomatically,
police call ended.

Angel Face exits
to his bicycle. Helmet on,
still calling out abuse.

The other side of the story.
'Shop stealer. His family too.
Abusive all.'

Angel Face,
where will you be in three years' time?
Prison? Mind the soap. You won't last long.

Those baby blues shoved up against
the shower room bowl.
Nothing will save your
tight angelic downy-covered anus hole.

Cruising Industrial Fortresses

Like industrial cruisers or medieval fortresses
the buildings sit in deep suburbia
along the one industrial street
within a stone's throw of neat
working-class houses
where the throb
at night
is loud.

The throb at night comes from generators
and fans that are at the heart of
this suburban industrial site
so close to these small
houses as to share
the same bird calls
and overhead
power lines.

Unchanged since World War II these industrial
monuments are a testament to
the great leap forward that
built a nation in a small
suburban way and come
sunset they power on
regardless even as
we sleep.

Sunset Industries

Woman. Late 70s.
Baseball cap. Floral blouse. Slacks.
Joggers. Carries a black garbage bag.
Gold necklace. Gold jewellery.
Well dressed.

She nods courteously
as I walk by her car
parked nearby.
Full garbage bags on the back seat.
Maybe she's part of a ladies bowling team?
No.
She is sorting out plastic bottles
from someone's bin,
not hers.

Man. Early 80s.
Push bike. Helmet. Shirt. Shorts. Joggers.
Part of a seniors cycling team out for the day?
No.
He has placed a line of cans on the asphalt,
crushing each, lifting each
into a cloth bag strapped to his bike.

Not a criticism of two seniors showing initiative,
but of a society that brings it on.

What will be next?
90-year-olds digging at the dump
for saleable items?
New sunset industries?
Seniors should be enjoying the fruits
of their many sunrises,
not fossicking through other people's rubbish.

I'm sorry, sir, I'm a bit slow

Coles supermarket.
Arndale Shopping Centre.
Saturday morning.
Rush hour.

The elderly woman
pushes her trolley
in front of me.

She stops.
She turns.
She says,
'I'm sorry, sir,
I'm a bit slow.'

She shuffles
off, haltingly.
My heart goes soft.
Nobody needs
to apologise
for who they are.

Later, I load
the Toyota with
three full shopping bags.
I see her shuffling
her trolley
across the car park,
alone, unassisted.

She must have been young, once.
Her spirit is still intact.
Independent.

Old woman, blue coat

A sight I never want to see again.

Old woman, blue coat, thick stockings,
thick glasses, walking stick,
wide-brimmed hat,
waiting for the lights to change.

For no apparent reason,
she steps slowly onto the asphalt
about to be covered by traffic
crossing the intersecting roads.

Lucky for her all traffic lights
have come to that twilight of the gods
when, for a split second,
there is a stillness as amber goes to red,
or amber goes to green.

Lucky for the old woman, blue coat.

I run fast forward, fully focused,
as does a woman on the opposite side.
Both put stop hands up.
Both halt the oncoming traffic.
Both gently touch a shoulder.

The traffic holds.
We guide this fragile old woman,
blue coat, safely across the road.

'I'm almost blind,' she says,
oblivious to the parting of the Red Sea
that has miraculously let her escape
the Pharaoh's oncoming death machines.

They should shoot people like me

Ancient couple. He, just parked their Ford.
She, trying to negotiate her walker.
He, 'Can you help us cross this busy road
to the surgery? Kindness is its own reward.'

Main road's morning traffic is not tame.
Two lanes each way. This is no video game.

The journey begins. The Universe smiles.
A gap in the traffic. Each step seems miles.
We propel the walker slowly
to the narrow medium strip.
We wait. The Universe smiles again.
Another break in the killer traffic. Amen!

She, 'They should shoot people like me.'
Where lies the future for he and she?

My hand raises as a Stop sign.
Haltingly, we continue our design.
The other-side pavement is barely made
before arrival of the car, bus and truck brigade.
Release. A small hesitate.
Cracked cement leads to the surgery gate.

Then we are there, relief is palpable.
Soft hand shakes all round, remarkable.
Will the Universe smile as before,
as later, they risk death once more?

Later. The return.
Two frail seniors journey in reverse.
Will their blood be spattered
on the road?

Diamonds not forever

Misty morning.
Dew-encrusted tree.
Spring shoots.
In one small corner
one small spider
has spun
a crown-jewelled web.

Diamonds not forever.
In swift saw cuts,
the small tree,
glistening web,
and spider,
all cut down
and fed into the
mulcher.

Ad Victor Spolia

Oh valiant chariot with
two cutting blades.
Ben Hur's opponents couldn't
do it better.

Power on. In full flight,
wondrous to behold. Your courage
shines. You slash. Decimate
your enemies. No prisoners!

Today, dear chariot of fire,
I tease you into action
to the glory you aspire.
Pull. No go. Pull. No go.

Five pulls. Ten.
No life. A wiser man
once said, 'Persist.' Pull.
You spring to life. Victorious Victa!

Is there a twist?

While blading down
the agro out front soursobs
and thinking of an early lunch,
a nearby neighbour interrupts,
'Will you cut my grass? I'll
pay.' Done. And then another.
Done and paid for.

I then reflect,
'To the victor go the spoils.
The Victa wins the moolah, just persist,
persist,   persist!'

First splashes

They bounce.
Two young African girls
bouncing, bouncing,
laughing in Sudanese,
next door on their trampoline,
unaware of gathering dark
rain clouds atop Mount Lofty,
coming to dampen their enthusiasm.

The rain, when it comes,
will be cold, drenching, heavy as lead.

'Leave now!'
I want to shout across the fence.
'Escape to safety!'

First splashes hit their young faces
as they gather their stuff and run
from the trampoline into the house,
screaming with girlish delight.

The soursobs can't run,
can't hide, have nowhere to go.
They must weather the storm regardless.
The rain, lethal as a hail of bullets
in North Sudan on fragile young brown bodies.
The soursobs will be
mowed down by the Victa
come the next fine day.

The girls?

Trampoline bouncing,
unaware of the trauma left behind them
in Sudan from whence their father fled
through Egypt to Australia, to Adelaide,
before they were born,
before they too could be
mowed down by the
victors in their homeland,
North Sudan.

Unnatural Assignation

Dear sweet old lady, you
remind me of Gloria Swanston
in *Sunset Boulevard*
as you sweep onto
the front porch in your
elegant brown cape with the
turquoise eyelinered eyes.
Edwardian silk design, maybe
an original Vande Waar
or maybe a reproduction by
the Aleni Brothers.

I'd invite you in, my dear,
but I know your stay will be brief.
You have other suitors
that you flirt with in your
shy coquettish but always
vigilant old lady way.
You turn me on.

Our last assignation was
as brief, delicious, or maybe
that was your twin sister. There
is a family resemblance.
I suspect you fool we simple humans
with your dark charms, this way.

Rest a moment, dear sweet lady,
in the shade. No one will
disturb you. No yapping
dog will sniff you, bite you.
There are no peeping toms here,
my darling one.

What's that, dear lady?
You want to stay all day.
What will the neighbours say?
No matter. I will suffer the
consequences of the gossip
about our strange unnatural
assignation against all human
decency, dear old lady. You
remind me of my…
let's not go there.

Of course. And stay all day
in the shade. Cool. As long as…
and she flutters away.

Old lady moth,
Dasypodia selenophora to be
correct. A real Latin lover.
Be safe. When will we meet
again, Dasy? Or your sister,
cousin, lookalike moths in
their elegant brown capes with the
turquoise eyelinered eyes.

I will again show human kindness
now that we have been so formally
introduced after heeling you
with my boot all these years.

Just my fear of moths.

Some humans fear
spiders and some
fear snakes.

Dunny Snake

My sister's shrill scream was loud and long
as she ran for her life from the dunny
outside our caretakers' place behind
Bishop's Lodge on the side of Castle Hill,
Townsville, North Queensland.

Mum was the first to arrive on the scene
followed quickly by Dad with shovel in hand.
He'd a fair inkling of what she had grabbed
instead of the chain, for Mum had
yanked the snake chain the previous week.

After a whopping great thwack, he emerged
smiling with snake dangling from hand.
A python for sure, long and thin, very dead,
probably ratting but wrong place to go
for a feed. Now shovel sent to Snake Heaven.

Out came the camera, we all stood around,
and Dad held the snake, smiling, looking pleased
with himself at the length of the brute.
Mum also smiling. A story to tell to the Bishop,
maybe to use in a sermon on Adam and Eve.

But no Cobber, my loving black and white kelpie
ever faithful as a guard dog. This time not ready.
Maybe chasing a kanga down the side of The Hill.
I loved my dear Cobber as a shy kid of seven,
with many a fun time shared on bush tracks.

At our next house he was mortally paw-bitten
by a snake that escaped. He died madly
yelping in frenzied lounge room circles
before Dad had to shovel his head.
We buried him at the side of the creek.

Never had a dog since my one and only
best friend Cobber, and always very wary
of snakes whether pythons or brownies.
Good memories last longer than childhood
and don't sepia-fade like old photographs.

Sheep Eyes

Almost gridlocked. Bumper to bumper.
Oppressive.
I don't need such oppression
on a hot Friday afternoon.

The livestock transporter thunders
to a crawl beside my car.
The lights turn red.
We both slow to a halt.

A sideways glance.
Sheep.
Main South Road.
Peak hour traffic.
Oppressive.

Oppressive, but,
sheep.
Levels 1,2,3,4.
Sheep,
packed tightly within each level.
Hundreds of sheep.

Sheep eyes
sad, questioning.
Lambs. Ewes.
All standing, shivering.
Stench.
Going from where to nowhere.
A bloody abattoir.

The standing.
The shivering. The eyes.
The sadness in the eyes.

These sheep have done no wrong.
Why should they suffer
such human callousness?

Seven thousand tigers

I was dapping through the archives
21st century, olden days,
when I came across this cryptic note,
'Seven thousand tigers left.'
Long time before my birth,
they'd all been killed.

Dad says,
'Stick to generic brands, son.'
So when the food tube came
I read the label, what a shock.
'Some ingredients are natural.'
I threw it out, damn quick!

Mum says,
'Artificial's safe and norm,
natural is bad.
Just remember my advice, son,
always eat what's in a can,
or zap it with your gamma gun.'

Uncle Bill says,
'When the world's zoos closed,
the animals were minced.
Pets were eaten by their owners.
Animal lib is dead.
Three cheers for common sense.'

I would like to own a human pet.
Next year they pass a law
that will allow us chosen ones
to buy them from a store.
I can't wait to get mine.
Dad's already built a cage.

Cars now in the past.
Old roads are just for walking on.
Those that cannot walk
are euthanased
at roadside dumps,
but have your permit ready.
Maybe you can tell me,
'What's a tiger?'

Standing in the pit

When I was eight, we lived in Townsville
in a run-down Housing Commission house
on stumps. Mum, Dad, my older sister,
baby brother, me,
and Cobber my beloved kelpie.

He died of a fit
running round the lounge room.
We buried him in the back garden.
A big, gentle dog. Dead.

In nearby scrub, my sister and I
watched brolgas dance.
We swam the Tobruk Memorial Pool
where Dawn Fraser trained
for the Olympic Games.

Good times if you don't count
Mum trying to commit suicide
in the storm water pit
at the side of the house,
my sister pleading her not to.
Me, unseen, eight, squatting,
watching, through the house stumps.
Maybe just a cry for help.
There wasn't enough water in the pit
to drown even a small child.

Life was hard for Mum,
Dad always on the road, a PMG technician.
Mum looking after us three kids, alone
for months on end.

Mum's stroke at 42.
Her life was fraught.
Mum standing in the pit.

A cry for help?

The Spanning Years

January 10th 1938.
Mum (not Mum then)
writes to Dad (her boyfriend),
Palestine Police Force,
terrorist dossier compiler,
official photographer.
A bitter-sweet letter,
'Love me or leave me',
ending with,
'I have spread my dreams under your feet;
Tread softly because you tread on my dreams.'

Did the trick. They married in December 1939.
Never an easy marriage.

When she wrote the letter, not quite 25.
When he received it, not quite 28.

January 10th 2015
77 years later,
I am reading *The Works of W.B. Yeats*.
The poem, 'He wishes for the Cloths of Heaven'.
Final line,
'I have spread my dreams under your feet;
Tread softly because you tread on my dreams.'

I sit here, in this chair,
in Dad and Mum's old house,
where I now live,
thrown back in time
to 1938.

2004, Mum died at 91.
Just before she died, Mum whispered, 'Son,
he was the only man I ever loved.'

I'm glad she was once
so young and innocent.
When did life's harsh reality set in?
And he? As young and innocent as she.

Father and Son

Listening to some Philip Glass piano
flowing from the car's CD player
as I drift away at the top
of the boat ramp
Outer Harbor.

Time passes.
Yawn.
Upright the seat.

A father and son are standing
on the boat ramp below.
The boy is tossing stones into the sea.
The father shows him
how to skim them further.

I think of Dad.
The tears well up.
I wonder why he never taught me
how to skim stones across the sea.
Skim or sink,
either
would have been just fine.

He did once try
to teach me to play cricket
on the next door oval.
I said emphatically, 'No!'

Silly boy.

A seagull looks at me with one eye,
'Silly man.'

The father and son
move to the top of the ramp.
The father continues sharing knowledge
with his son.

My father lately,
although a long time dead,
is on my mind again.
He shares his knowledge freely
from the grave.
He teaches me to be a man
as I stand and talk with him,
visit by visit,
at the edge of the water
lapping the boat ramp
at Outer Harbor.
My silent sounding board.

I guess that's as good
as learning how to play cricket
or skimming stones.
A pelican floats by and seems to stare,
'You got that right, mate.'

And burnt to death

Anger? Love? Hate?
Only the perpetrator will truly ever know,
and I, the car that screamed and burnt to death.
The TV film crew never can report the facts,
only show my twisted burnt out body.
The perpetrator? He, long fled. And I?
Already burnt to death.

Stripped naked in a foreign street,
my guts ripped out, my eyes, shards across
the cooling asphalt. You were my friend, lover,
soulmate. Now I'm an unloved shell
that dogs will lift their legs and piss against.

You insatiably unlocked my inner being;
came inside me; thrust your feet
on my affections; caressed my power
for selfish needs; abandoned me,
a fiery furnace; fled the scene of your depraved
and witless act. And I? Alone. Distressed.
I died a fiery death as flames engulfed my all,
and in my death throws, screaming, 'Why?'

Did you grow weary, need a change?
Will the end of your new lover lie
in some foreign street like me? Gutted
in the flames of hate, or man-boy angst.

You vapid mongrel cur who bought me
cheap, then, when done, petrol doused
me, killing the very spirit
that you, in your perverted way,
coveted above all else.

Have you beguiled, befriended, bought
a sleeker, newer, faster car in which
to pedal thrust your animal desires?

This siren call to all my sisters, friends
and lovers, just beware. Your time is brief.
You will be used; abandoned; stripped naked;
disembowelled; crushed; or burnt to death.
True love is rare and happens over time
to but a few who have the vintage classic
look or spirit strong.

Did you hate your father or your mother?
Why take it out on me?

At times like this

(at death's door)

you think of women
never slept with
or men if that's
your inclination way.

Of fights you should
have cared for,
or stood for causes
on their defining day.

Or children whom you
never sired or helped
to understand the path
for their fulfilment.

At times like this,
the money never present,
friendships never thought
to foster or to grow.

You think of endings
and disasters, or sadly
fading fast unfinished
or unloved and low.

But stop and ponder,
no need to weep
or fail to view the
wonders you've achieved.

Know that you have
around you people
real or virtual
who are there, I vow.

And wealth aplenty
in nature's eye to
the beauty of the sunset,
the sunrise, all between.

Put away your
pain and sadness
of where you were
as best you can.

Reach out into the
newness of seeing
all things fresh,
nature, woman, man.

Men, women, young folk,
we all can plummet
low. Look around you
to appreciate life's simple glow.

Love yourself
to love another,
and let the rivers flow.

Unending Sadness

Bleaker than the Gobi Desert
come the noonday anvil sun.

Colder than Oates leaving the tent
and Scott's men freezing to death.

Humanity unending as the door opens
and closes. Seats grubby green insensitive.

Where is this haven, not, of dreams?
Centrelink, Kilkenny, Friday afternoon.

Was here this morn before it opened,
to avoid the crush, or so I hoped, but

P&L Statement requested. Home. Done.
10 minutes flat. Return. And then the wait.

Tired faces. Counter staff doing their best
to be cheery, generous, considerate. Hard.

'You tell us not to be rude,' snaps a woman,
frustrated she didn't get a quick reply.

I nod to the security guard, Indian,
he mouths, '2 ½ hours to go. Here since 8.30 a.m.'

A long time to stand, just shifting your feet.
The queue keeps growing. No end in sight.

'Martin?' The voice of God? No. Counter staff
ready to process my P&L Statement.

Scanned. Date stamped. Signed.
I'm out of there quick smart, be sure of that!

The gentle rain droppeth from Heaven
as Shakespeare's Portia sayeth. Couth!

The others wait in hope that their release
will be as swift, and cleanly ended.

Centrelink, Kilkenny. Home of the dreary.
Land of the brave.

In Australia, my voice identifies me

Taking a break. Back garden bench.

An Australian Crested Pigeon
flies in, settles by the
Norfolk Island hibiscus tree,
eyes enquiring, nervous head twitch.
I can't resist the urge.

Return with half a slice of wholemeal bread.
Call, 'Brd, brd.' No response.
Then lower my height,
squat a pace or two
from the bird.

ACP silently pads towards the bread bits
sussing out the massive
Brd brd being, begins to nibble cautiously.

I think, 'A fluke.'
Inner voice, 'Go beyond this first time.'
Did.

For a week now, I see ACP settling near
the tree, waiting.
Out I go with bread in hand,
low 'Brd, brd' call.

ACP responds
with a throaty single 'Vrr.'
Lets me get closer to
the food tree. Its single 'Vrr'
reassures me
the bread is going
to a worthy gullet.

ACP's mate flutters in
for her feed too.

In Australia, my voice identifies me.
Centrelink, that's one thing
you sure got right!

Natural Selection

Early morning suburban trek.
Two magpies standing still.

I summon up the gods.
Artemis, Actaeon and Pan.

The Druid within channels.
'Yaa-er, Yaa-er' in fluent magpie.

They look at each other.
'Dickhead, dickhead' is all I hear.

They fly off   impressively.

Loo break with Aunty ABC

The wallpaper stripping exercise
was a breeze,
just the stubborn flecks remaining.
A quick piss.

Slopping on the stripper,
listening to Aunty ABC and her
sensuous classical music.

In a nanosecond
the tall metal ladder
        with me at the top
                slid down
                        crashing into the loo cistern
                            shattering it.

Continued its journey
(with me at the top)
        to the loo pan
                cracked it.

Stopped.

The water,
released from the cistern,
cascaded over me
onto the green cement floor.
Time didn't stand still but sped up.

There were shattered cistern parts
scattered all over the floor.
>	Water.
>>	Paste.
>>>	Goo.

Blood.

All I could see was a gash
in my left palm.
Lucky I didn't cut my thumb off,
or worse.

Up quickly, fast examination,
no other damage, except for
a shin bump that was bruising quickly,
and a flattened male ego.

Aunty's voice was oozing on regardless.

Thanks, Aunty. It could have been worse.
At least I wasn't head banging!

Thanks, APIA, for the new loo.

I'll think of you both
>	when next
>>	I piss.

Vale ladder

Shiny new. Bunnings.
Just after Dad died.
To begin renovating
Mum's place.

Stairway to Heaven?
Well, at least the roof,
guttering, trees,
always ready
for active duty.

You could have left me
on the roof, inside the roof,
or clinging to a tree.
Faithful till the end.

Last week,
putting you against
the fence, you creaked,
just fell apart.
Vale, old friend.

Now what to do with
the bloody thing!
For now, behind the shed.
Maybe the god of
ladders will take pity,
whisk you up to
Ladder Heaven.

Old soldiers fade away,
the same for you?

Small Egos Travelling

Woman at lights
delicately lipsticking her lips
and at the next set
going through a red one.

Man adjusting tie
ever so careful with the knot
takes his foot off brake
and car edges into another.

Kids in the back
squabbling over a smart phone game
till one face-hits the other
and pandemonium breaks out.

Individual small egos
travelling who knows where
on a daily basis
into oblivion.

Small Life Force Voyager

Suddenly aware
of a small moth
beating its Magellan journey
through lounge room space
just in front of
my gesticulating finger.

So near and steady
beside my now stilled finger
as to be a satellite
around a huge planet
that easily could have seized it up
had I not been transfixed
by this small life force voyager
claiming the Universe of space
that stretched around it.

Magellan and Columbus,
Gagarin, Shepherd, Armstrong,
Mariner and *Voyager*.
Beginning acts of faith.

We are all that small life force voyager
fluttering our fragile wings
through the vast uncharted
Universe of Life.

Acknowledgements

'Outback ruin': *Red River Review*, USA, 2018;
Frances 20th Anniversary Anthology, 2019
'Chatting with Fellini': *Verse Wrights*, USA, 2017
'No Through Road': *StepAway Magazine*, UK, 2017;
The Deeper Inner, Ginninderra Press Pocket Poets, 2017
'How does the saying go?': *Friendly Street Reader* 39, 2015
'Ya, ya, ya': *Illya's Honey*, USA, 2017
'Western Suburb Heaven': *InDaily*, 2016
'Chainsaw Massacre': *Pure Slush*, 2019
'Old woman, blue coat': *The Deeper Inner*, Ginninderra Press Pocket Poets, 2017
'Sheep Eyes': *Gawler Poetry Reader* Number 6, 2013
'Seven thousand tigers': *Red River Review*, USA, 2018
'The Spanning Years': *Friendly Street Reader* 40, 2016
'And Burnt To Death': *Friendly Street Reader* 41, 2017
'Natural Selection': *Bindweed Magazine*, 2019
'Small Life Force Voyager': *Friendly Street Reader* 38, 2014;
Frances 20th Anniversary Anthology, 2019

About the Author

Martin Christmas's parents immigrated to Australia at the end of the 1940s. He grew up in North Queensland; briefly in the UK during a return visit; and in Adelaide, South Australia.

He first worked in a government accounting office before quitting and going into the arts. He has spent most of his adult life working as a theatre director in South Australia and Victoria, and as drama teacher, mainly in South Australia. He has a BA in Theatre Studies and an MA in Cultural Studies.

Always lurking in the background was his fascination with spoken word and poetic imagery. In 2010 he threw out most of his poetry (which he had been writing since high school). In 2011 he read a couple of surviving poems at a Friendly Street Poets open mic session and was drawn into the world of poetry.

These days, as well as performing his poetry, he runs one to one and group workshops in spoken word presentation (his experience as a theatre director has come in very handy). He also photographs spoken word events and urban landscapes.

He has been published in the Friendly Street Poets Reader since 2012, in several Australian online and print magazines, and in online journals in the USA and the UK. Ginninderra Press has published both his chapbooks, *Immediate Reflections* and *The Deeper Inner*. In July 2019, Ginninderra Press published *D&M Between 2 Men*, a shared poetry book with Andrew Drake.

Random Adventures is his first full length poetry book.

www.ingramcontent.com/pod-product-compliance
Lightning Source LLC
Chambersburg PA
CBHW070931080526
44589CB00013B/1473